Bankruptcy: The Path to Recovery

Randall R. Saxton

Saxton Law, PLLC
www.saxton.law

Madison, MS

CONTENTS

CHAPTER ONE

INTRODUCTION

PLEASE NOTE: As you read through this book, I encourage you to make notes, so you can ask questions during your free consultation with my office. I am providing this information to help you understand the bankruptcy process and to provide helpful information that will assist you as you recover and rebuild after a financial hardship.

Congress enacted bankruptcy laws to help people who can no longer pay their debts. The law provides a way to give the person a "fresh start" by liquidating assets to pay debts or creating a repayment plan to pay debts. In most cases, debtors don't have assets that are subject to liquidation in a Chapter 7 case, therefore, the debts are simply discharged. In other words, the debtor is no longer legally liable to repay those debts.

The Supreme Court stated the fundamental goal of bankruptcy in its decision in Local Loan Co. v. Hunt, 292

U.S. 234, 244 (1934). In its decision, the court stated that bankruptcy "gives to the honest but unfortunate debtor…a new opportunity in life and a clear field for future effort, unhampered by the pressure and discouragement of pre-existing debt." The justices made it clear that bankruptcy was not only intended to wipe away old debt but give the debtor a way to rebuild his or her finances.

Bankruptcy is often the last resort people choose in order to deal with their financial problems. It's hard to believe that anyone would voluntarily choose to declare bankruptcy unless it was absolutely necessary. Unfortunately for some people, filing bankruptcy is the only effective resolution to their debt problems. Bankruptcy is not something to be entered into lightly. It is not the "easy way" out of debt that some people believe it to be. While filing bankruptcy will give you the opportunity to build a better financial future for you and your family, declaring bankruptcy can make life quite a bit harder for a short while. Hiring an experienced bankruptcy attorney to guide you through the bankruptcy process can make filing for bankruptcy relief much smoother and a lot less stressful.

Many people who file bankruptcy don't understand they can rebuild their credit after the bankruptcy case is complete. Most people believe bankruptcy is a terrible black mark that you carry around with you forever. This is not true. While bankruptcy will remain on your credit for a few years, the good news is that filing a bankruptcy case often helps you rebuild your credit much faster than ignoring your debt problem and hoping it will eventually go away.

Once you file a bankruptcy case, it may be more difficult to obtain credit for major purchases such as houses and vehicles. It may be difficult, but not impossible. That's is one of the purposes of filing bankruptcy — to rebuild your good credit standing so that you can qualify for credit in the future at a reasonable interest rate. It is a bankruptcy myth that people who file a bankruptcy case never own another home, buy a new vehicle, or take a family vacation. Many people find that they can rebuild their credit for a bright and successful financial future.

This book is intended to be a guide for rebuilding credit after filing bankruptcy. You will learn several key concepts that you can use as you decide and find life after bankruptcy including:

- What is bankruptcy?
- Why do people file for bankruptcy relief?
- The steps you can take to rebuild your credit after filing bankruptcy.
- How filing bankruptcy can be a positive step in establishing financial freedom and a healthy financial well-being.

Although bankruptcy is a last resort for many people who are unable to pay their creditors, bankruptcy doesn't have to be the end of your financial well-being. You can rebuild your credit after filing bankruptcy, and I am going to show you how to do it!

CHAPTER TWO

GETTING OUT OF DEBT – NOT FUN, BUT NOT IMPOSSIBLE

Getting into debt is easy; it is getting out of debt that is difficult. This section provides an explanation of the various options you may have for getting rid of your debt.

1) TAKE ADVANTAGE OF YOUR ASSETS

If you have assets that have significant equity, such as a home or a car, you may be able to use these assets as a way to deal with your debt. For example, you might could get a loan for your home that is large enough to pay off your debts. You can save a great deal of money in interest payments if you pay off high-interest credit card debt. If you have a car, you can consider selling your vehicle to pay off debts and purchase a used vehicle. However, there are some things you must seriously consider before using this alternative to filing bankruptcy.

Purchasing a used car may cost you more in repairs, and fuel costs so beware. A more serious concern is in mortgaging your home to pay unsecured debt. If you are unable to pay the mortgage payment, you lose your home because you turned unsecured debt (i.e. credit card debt) into a secured debt. The credit card company won't be able to take your home if you don't pay the credit card company but the mortgage company can foreclose on the mortgage and take your home for failure to pay the payments. You must seriously think about this option before you take any action. Consulting with a bankruptcy attorney BEFORE taking any action is your best option for protecting your assets.

2) INCREASE YOUR INCOME

Getting a second job can provide the additional income you need to pay off debt. Make a list of your debts and interest rates. Pay off the debts with the highest rates first and work your way down the list. This may sound tedious, but sometimes it is necessary. Remember, working a second job is not forever, and it can prevent your credit rating from taking a hit because of late payments, repossessions, or a bankruptcy case.

3) PUT A HOLD ON YOUR CREDIT CARDS

One of the best steps you can take to get out of debt is to stop adding to the debt. Credit cards are an amazingly easy way to add to your debts, as most of us don't see credit cards for the problems that they pose to our budget. I would suggest keeping only one credit card for emergencies. Remember, credit is not an inherently evil concept when used wisely. In fact, it is good to have a credit card that you use and pay off regularly to keep your credit rating higher. Creditors want to see responsible use of credit when deciding whether to lend money to you. However, if credit cards are too tempting, you may need to close all but one for now until you develop good money management skills. (HINT: The debtor education courses required when you file bankruptcy provide useful information and teach skills you can use to manage your credit and money wisely. You don't have to be in bankruptcy to take these courses.)

4) SET UP A REPAYMENT PLAN

Cut back on your expenses as much as possible and use the extra cash to repay your debts. Pay off debts with the highest rates first and work your way down the list. In order to make this work, you do need to create and live within a monthly budget. Think of a budget as a way to get the things you want rather than a punishment. A budget allows you to see where your money is going each month to plug up any "holes" that are allowing your income to escape each month.

5) CONSOLIDATION LOAN

A consolidation loan can help you out of debt without declaring bankruptcy, but I say this with a bit of caution as explained above. A consolidation loan is used to pay off all debts so that you have one monthly payment for those debts. The new loan typically has a smaller payment and a lower interest rate. If you can do this, without jeopardizing your assets with a secured loan, you may want to consider an unsecured consolidation loan before filing bankruptcy. Again, make it an UNSECURED loan and make sure you can afford the payment or it defeats its purpose.

6) HIRE A CREDIT COUNSELOR

Some people say they have had great success in getting out of debt when using a credit counselor while other people have said it was the worst financial decision they ever made. The lesson to be learned — be extremely careful when searching for and hiring a credit counselor. Some so-called credit counselors are in business to make a profit for themselves more so than to help their clients get out of debt.

You can choose from two types of credit counselors — for-profit credit counselors and non-profit credit counselors. They do the same job, and they both charge a fee. Credit counselors can help you by teaching you how to get control of your debt, by helping you devise a plan to pay off debts, and by helping you create and learn to live within a budget. You must do your homework before hiring a credit counselor to ensure you are receiving the best value for your money.

Many people don't fully understand the ramifications involved in using a credit counselor. Some common questions I answer regarding using a credit counselor include:

> ➤ *How will it affect my credit rating?*

If the credit counselor assists you in negotiating a repayment plan for one or more of your creditors, the creditor will most likely report this information to the credit bureau. The credit bureau will record that a plan is in place and the impact of this notation may lower your credit score.

> ➤ *Are your payments too high?*

Your payments should be large enough to help you reduce your debt but not so high that you have nothing left over each month to place money into an emergency savings account and pay your necessary living expenses. If your payment is too high, you risk the need of obtaining additional credit for a financial crisis, or you miss the payment because you don't have enough money left over at the end of the month after paying living expenses to make the payment. If a credit counselor doesn't prepare a monthly budget, teach you how to prepare a budget, and encourage you to always live within a budget, beware and move on to another option.

> *Do creditors have to work with my credit counselor?*

No, creditors are not forced to work with your credit counselor. Therefore, you may find that your plan to get out of debt is not feasible.

> *Why do I pay a fee for a non-profit credit counselor?*

The fee for a non-profit credit counselor is to cover necessary costs of the counselor and the company. The company is a non-profit; therefore, it is not allowed to earn profits. It can only cover its costs. Make sure it is an actual non-profit recognized by the government. A for-profit credit counselor is in business to make money. In addition to charging a fee to cover expenses, the counselor and company charge a fee that is designed to earn a profit.

7) INFORMAL AGREEMENTS- TIMELY PAYMENT AGREEMENT

In some cases, you can arrange a payment agreement with your creditors to set up a repayment plan that allows you to pay them back over a given period of time. This helps preserve your credit rating — only if the creditor stops reporting late payments, not all creditors agree to stop reporting negative information.

8) INFORMAL LUMP SUM AGREEMENT.

You may be able to pay less than 100 cents on the dollar if you choose to take this route. For example, you may pay a lump sum to the creditor of 50% of the amount owed to settle the debt. The remaining 50% of the debt owed is "written off" by the creditor. Of course, you must have access to funds that allow you to pay the lump sum payments. WARNING: Creditors who write off debt are obligated to report those debts to the IRS at the end of the year. You are issued a 1099 and must report the canceled debt as income on your tax return. Reporting canceled debt as income can lower your tax refund or result in owing taxes. Discuss the matter with a tax attorney or tax consultant if you have substantial debt that will be written off under this option.

9) FILING FOR BANKRUPTCY RELIEF

If you have tried all other options for getting out of debt or the remaining options after trying several options aren't practical for you, then filing bankruptcy may be your best option for resolving your debt problem.

You are probably a good candidate for filing a Chapter 13 bankruptcy if any of the following situations apply:

- You have a real and sincere desire to repay your debts, but you need the protection of the bankruptcy court to do so.

- You are behind on your mortgage or car loan and want to make up the missed payments over time. Chapter 7 bankruptcy doesn't allow you do this. You can catch up missed payments in a Chapter 13 bankruptcy plan to keep your home and car.

- You are a family farmer who wants to pay off your debts, but you don't qualify for a Chapter 12 family farming bankruptcy because you have a large debt unrelated to farming.

- You have valuable property that is not exempt under the bankruptcy exemptions and would be in jeopardy if you filed a Chapter 7 bankruptcy case.

- You received a Chapter 7 discharge within the past four years.

- You have someone who is in debt with you. If you file for Chapter 7 bankruptcy, your creditor will go after the co-signer for payment of the debt.

- You have a tax debt. If a large part of your debt consists of personal income taxes, a Chapter 13 case allows you to spread out the portion of taxes that are non-dischargeable over a 60-month plan. This is also the case if you owe back child support or alimony.

- You don't meet the income requirements under the means test to file bankruptcy under Chapter 7.

You are probably a good candidate for filing a Chapter 7 bankruptcy if the following situations apply:

- You meet the income requirements of the means test for filing under Chapter 7.

- You don't have any income left over at the end of the month to pay debts after you pay your normal living expenses.

- You have substantial unsecured debt, such as credit card debt, medical bills, and personal loans.

- You don't have any assets that would be non-exempt in a bankruptcy filing.

- Your source of income is from Social Security, retirement, or disability income.

CHAPTER THREE

UNDERSTANDING THE INS AND OUTS OF BANKRUPTCY

When you choose to file a bankruptcy case to resolve debts you can no longer afford to pay, you should have sound legal counsel guiding you in your decision. The decision to file a bankruptcy case should not be taken lightly. Bankruptcy is a serious matter that can impact the way creditors view your financial stability for several years after you've received your bankruptcy discharge and your case has been closed.

Bankruptcy is not an "easy out" for those who are overwhelmed by debt. However, bankruptcy is intended to help individuals who simply can't see another way out of debt and who don't have the means to pay their debts.

RECENT BANKRUPTCY CHANGES

Article I, Section 8 of the United States Constitution gives Congress the power to enact uniform bankruptcy laws. The first Bankruptcy Act was passed in 1800 but it, like others passed after it, were short-lived and eventually repealed by Congress until the Bankruptcy Reform Act of 1978 was passed. The 1978 Act established bankruptcy courts and allowed for the appointment of bankruptcy judges. The following year, the U.S. Trustee pilot program was established. Bankruptcy laws were amended slightly over the years until 2005 when sweeping changes were made when Congress passed the Bankruptcy Abuse Prevention and Consumer Protection Act of 2005. BAPCPA substantially amended the 1978 Act by adding a means test and making credit counseling and debtor education a condition for receiving bankruptcy relief.

PROS AND CONS OF FILING BANKRUPTCY

As discussed above, filing for bankruptcy relief is a serious matter that should not be taken lightly. While bankruptcy may get rid of most, if not all, of your debt, there are consequences for filing bankruptcy. For most people who are unable to pay their debts because they don't have any money left over at the end of each month after paying their living expenses, the benefits of filing bankruptcy typically outweigh the consequences. Also, as I discussed above, the effects of filing bankruptcy are usually temporary, and you can overcome them with persistence and time.

Bankruptcy is best for someone with considerable debts, no income, and no assets. The people it has the highest effect on are those that have equity in property, disposable income, people who have certain professional qualifications because they stand to lose the most when filing for bankruptcy relief. However, filing for relief is sometimes the best option regardless of whether the person may stand to lose some assets. Giving up a little to get rid of thousands of dollars in debt is often better than facing foreclosures, repossessions, wage garnishments, and personal judgments.

Pros of filing bankruptcy include:

- Discharge of most, if not all, unsecured debts, including credit card debt, medical bills, and personal loans

- Stops foreclosures and repossessions

- Stops credit harassment

- Allows you to protect assets

- Provides a fresh start free from debt

- Bankruptcy exemptions protect some property from the court and creditors

Cons of filing bankruptcy include:

- May lose some assets

- Remains on your credit history for 7 to 10 years

- Can possibly result in a temporary decrease in credit scores

- Doesn't discharge all debts (i.e. alimony, child support, student loans, and some taxes)

ALTERNATIVES TO FILING FOR BANKRUPTCY

There are several alternatives to filing for bankruptcy relief. The first is to ignore the problem. Obviously, this is an extremely BAD alternative that can result in foreclosures, repossessions, personal judgments, and wage garnishments. I strong advise against this option. It is never a wise choice to ignore debt problems.

Another alternative is to obtain a personal loan or a secured loan to consolidate your debt. This may work if you have sufficient income to repay the consolidation loan. However, there are some disadvantages in choosing this alternative to bankruptcy. The first problem is affording the debt payment. If you are already struggling to pay your debts, consolidating the debts into one monthly payment may seem wise, but if you don't have the income to pay the debt, you are just switching one problem for another problem. Furthermore, if you choose to secure the debt, you are putting your property at risk. For example, if you choose a second mortgage to consolidate credit card debt, you are switching unsecured debts for a secured debt. If you cannot pay the mortgage payments, you risk losing your home.

Many people turn to debt consolidation companies for help. These companies promise to negotiate with your creditors to reduce your payments and combine your debt into one low monthly payment you can afford. There are also several problems with this bankruptcy alternative. One, you must pay the company for this service. The fees for a debt consolidation company can be very high. Second, your creditors are not obligated to participate in this debt consolidation. Therefore, you may have several creditors that continue to pursue you for the debts that you owe, including filing collection lawsuits or seeking repossession of assets. Third, your creditors continue to report late payments and negative information on your credit history and may continue to harass you for payments.

On the other hand, filing a bankruptcy case forces all creditors to work with you to resolve your debt. Creditors cannot "opt out" of bankruptcy and must seek bankruptcy court approval before taking any action to collect a debt outside of your bankruptcy case. In most Chapter 7 bankruptcy cases, the debtor gets rid of most, if not all, of his debt while keeping all his property. In a Chapter 13 bankruptcy case, the debtor keeps his property while setting up an affordable monthly payment plan to resolve debt problems.

In many cases, filing a bankruptcy case is the best option for resolving a debt problem. However, it is in your best interest to consult with an experienced bankruptcy attorney before deciding to file a bankruptcy case. An attorney helps you determine if bankruptcy is your best alternative for resolving a debt problem, and if so, what chapter of bankruptcy you should file. Once you decide to file a bankruptcy case, your attorney walks you through the process of filing the case to ensure that everything is handled correctly.

CHAPTER FOUR

THE BANKRUPTCY PROCESS

If you are considering bankruptcy as a way to resolve your debt problem, it is absolutely necessary you seek legal advice from an experienced bankruptcy attorney. You can't go it alone and expect everything to work out in your best interest. Filing bankruptcy can be a complicated and complex undertaking, depending on the facts and circumstances of the case. When you file for bankruptcy, you want someone on your side who understands the bankruptcy process and bankruptcy laws to protect your best interest.

FILING A BANKRUPTCY CASE

In order to file for bankruptcy, you must file a bankruptcy petition, schedules, and statements. The court requires that you use the standard bankruptcy forms approved by the court. The forms include information regarding your assets, debts, income, expenses, and financial history in addition to personal information. You must list ALL assets and debts in your bankruptcy schedules — you cannot pick and choose what creditors will be included in your bankruptcy. However, different types of debt are treated in different ways and are listed in different sections of your bankruptcy schedules. This is another reason why you should hire an experienced bankruptcy attorney. Failing to list items in the proper section of your forms could result in debts being treated incorrectly.

You must also complete your credit counseling course before filing your bankruptcy petition. This course can be completed online, in person, or by telephone. The U.S. Trustee's office has a list of the approved credit counseling companies in your area. A certificate of completion must be filed with your bankruptcy petition. It reviews much of the same information you need to provide in your bankruptcy schedules. Before the end of your bankruptcy case, you must also complete a debtor education course and file the certificate with the court. If you fail to complete the second course, you will not receive a discharge, and you will continue to owe all debts as if you never filed the bankruptcy case.

After your bankruptcy is filed, the court will schedule your First Meeting of Creditors. This is an informal hearing with a bankruptcy trustee that lasts about 10 minutes. The trustee will ask questions regarding the information you included in your bankruptcy forms. Creditors may also appear and ask questions; however, very few creditors appear at these hearings. In a typical Chapter 7 bankruptcy case, this is the only hearing you will have in your case, and the case will be closed in four to six months. For a Chapter 13 case, you will also have a confirmation hearing that you may have to attend to confirm your proposed repayment plan.

The above information is a brief discussion of how to

file for bankruptcy, as this is a book about getting out from under bankruptcy's shadow. Below is a simple and brief discussion of Chapter 13 and Chapter 7 bankruptcy cases to give you an idea of how each case helps you get out of debt. For more detailed information about filing bankruptcy and the difference between a Chapter 13 and a Chapter 7 case, I encourage you to contact my office.

CHAPTER 13 BANKRUPTCY – THE PAYMENT PLAN

When someone files for bankruptcy under Chapter 13, the goal is to have the opportunity to repay some or all his or her debts through a manageable monthly plan of repayment. This is different from a Chapter 7 case that utilizes asset liquidation to repay creditors. Chapter 13 allows the debtor to use their income to pay their debts rather than selling off assets to repay creditors. Of course, a debtor must have a sufficient amount of steady monthly income to fund a Chapter 13 plan in order to qualify to file under this chapter of bankruptcy. While the attorney who represents you safeguards your interests, the entire process is carried out under the supervision of the courts and a Chapter 13 trustee who administers the case.

When you file your bankruptcy case, you include a proposed Chapter 13 plan. The plan sets forth how you intend to repay your creditors, and the plan has different sections for each type of creditor. For example, if you owe back mortgage or car payments, these debts are handled differently from medical bills and credit card debts. A Chapter 13 plan can be difficult to calculate; therefore, I highly recommend hiring an experienced bankruptcy attorney who can calculate a plan payment that is as low as possible but still meets the requirements set forth by the Bankruptcy Code.

The repayment plan must begin within thirty days after

the case is filed. You make your payments to a Chapter 13 trustee who then pays your creditor in accordance with the terms of the confirmed plan. Chapter 13 plans cannot exceed 60 months (5 years) and must pay a certain percentage to unsecured creditors (i.e. credit cards, medical bills, etc.) based on your disposable income (i.e. income less approved expenses). According to the law, creditors must strictly stick to the repayment plan that is approved by the court, and they can't pursue any collection efforts without court approval. Once you complete your bankruptcy plan, you receive a discharge. Most debts can be discharged through a Chapter 13 case. The exceptions to this rule include debts for alimony, child support, most student loans, and some taxes.

CHAPTER 7 BANKRUPTCY – THE LIQUIDATION PLAN

If filing for bankruptcy is an opportunity for a debtor to emerge out of a financial crisis with a fresh start, then Chapter 7 of the Bankruptcy Code is the way to do it a bit quicker. In order to qualify for Chapter 7, you must meet the income requirements of the means test. Chapter 7 is intended for people without a steady income or with an income that is not sufficient to pay debts after subtracting allowable living expenses.

Under Chapter 7, property considered non-exempt is sold, and the proceeds are distributed to creditors. Federal and state laws define the types and value of the property that a debtor can claim exempt under bankruptcy. This method of bankruptcy is also referred to as a liquidation bankruptcy because it turns assets into cash for the purpose of paying debt. Chapter 7 Bankruptcy is the most common form of bankruptcy and makes up about 65% of bankruptcy filings.

Chapter 7 is one of the faster ways to get out of debt

because most cases are completed within six months of the filing date. In a Chapter 7 bankruptcy case, a bankruptcy trustee takes possession of any non-exempt property, sells the assets, and distributes proceeds from the sale to creditors on your behalf. Even though most Chapter 7 cases are no-asset cases, meaning the debtor doesn't lose any assets, it is vital to consult with an experienced bankruptcy attorney before deciding to file this type of bankruptcy case. An added advantage with Chapter 7 bankruptcy is that by signing a reaffirmation agreement, a debtor can continue to pay a car loan to keep a vehicle. A reaffirmation agreement is not required to continue paying a mortgage.

An attorney *CANNOT* guarantee you won't lose any assets, but he can give you his opinion based on experience what he believes may happen when you file your case. However, you must be completely honest with your attorney. Hiding assets is a federal offense, and it makes it impossible for your attorney to provide you with sound legal advice regarding your case.

Under Chapter 7, the debtor receives a discharge of all dischargeable debts. Dischargeable debts include credit cards, medical bills, and most personal loans. Some taxes, most student loans, and domestic support are not dischargeable in bankruptcy, including Chapter 7 and Chapter 13 cases.

CHAPTER FIVE

GETTING STARTED REBUILDING CREDIT – PATIENCE IS A VIRTUE

One of the best things about receiving a fresh start on your credit by filing for bankruptcy is that it allows you a chance to rebuild your credit rating for a stronger financial well-being. However, it is important that I tell you that your credit rating won't improve as quickly when your old, negative information is shown on your credit history. Unfortunately, credit histories can be accessed by creditors for up to 10 years, even though some credit reports only show records for the past 36 or 60 months. The good news is that there are things you can do now to mitigate the negative information that has already been reported by creditors.

All three major credit reporting agencies know about you and your debts before you filed for bankruptcy. This information includes late payments, charge-offs, collections, over-the-limit notices, applications for credit, and judgments. After you receive a bankruptcy discharge, debts discharged in bankruptcy should be listed on your credit report as "Included in Bankruptcy." If an account isn't listed as included in bankruptcy, the account appears to be an active account in collection status, which will continue to damage your credit score and severely decrease your chance of getting new credit or new credit at a decent interest rate.

Unfortunately, creditors rarely report updates in credit records after a bankruptcy discharge. Therefore, a few months after your discharge, you should take the time to order copies of all three major credit reports to ensure your discharged debts are listed as being included in your bankruptcy. If you have not obtained free copies of your credit reports within the past 12 months, you are entitled to receive a free copy of your credit report from each of the three major reporting agencies. Go to AnnualCreditReport.com or call 1-877-322-8228 for information.

If you have received your free copy within the last 12 months, you can contact the three major credit reporting agencies directly to request a copy of your current credit report. Beware, you aren't required to purchase your credit score, credit monitoring, or credit repair assistance to purchase your credit report. You only want to purchase a copy of your current credit report because the other services offered by the agencies can be quite costly. The contact information for the three main credit reporting agencies are:

- Trans Union (800) 888-4213 or www.transunion.com
- Equifax (888) 397-3742 or www.Equifax.com
- Experian (800) 997-2493 or www.experian.com

In addition, here are a few more things that you can do to get your credit back in shape after bankruptcy:

❖ Give Yourself Credit

One of the best ways you can rebuild your credit rating after a bankruptcy is to establish credit accounts that report positive information to the credit reporting agencies. You will begin to receive credit applications a few months after your bankruptcy case is closed. The problem is that these accounts have high-interest rates attached to them because of your bankruptcy and the credit rating. However, payment history is the highest percentage of your credit score at 35% of the score. Therefore, apply for a well-known credit card with the lowest rate you can find and charge a small amount. Pay the monthly payment on time each month (pay more than the minimum payment if possible) until the amount is paid off then repeat the process. Another route you may consider is a secured credit card that I will discuss in another chapter.

❖ Read the Contract Small Print

You must know what you're getting into before you accept a credit offer. Make sure that you fully understand the interest rate and fees before you open a new credit account. Also, make sure you understand how the interest rate is calculated and how the minimum monthly payment is calculated. Many credit card companies offer anything to get you to open new credit accounts. However, many of these so-called great offers are introductory offers, and your payments and/or interest rates double within a few months after opening the account.

❖ Be Able to Prove Your Payments

Even after your debts are discharged through bankruptcy, you may need proof that you don't owe these creditors before you can establish credit again. Retain copies of your bankruptcy discharge order from the court and copies of your bankruptcy schedules that list the creditors included in your case so you can prove certain debts were listed in your bankruptcy and covered by your bankruptcy discharge. Having copies of your forms and your discharge is convenient and makes the job of re-establishing credit easier for you.

❖ Make All Payments on Time:

Most credit card companies and utilities report late payments to credit reporting agencies. If you make any late payments, future creditors see you as a bad credit risk. Also, you should note that most credit cards add a large late fee whenever you make a late payment that only increases the amount of money you owe on the credit card. Pay all payments, including debts and utility payments, on or before the due date. If you mail the payments, place the payment in the mail with enough time to arrive on or before the due date (5 to 7 days is usually sufficient for most locations).

TIP: Set up automatic drafts for regular monthly bills. This ensures that your payment will never be late.

CHAPTER SIX

MAKING BANKRUPTCY WORK FOR YOU – TURN A NEGATIVE INTO A POSITIVE

It may not seem like bankruptcy can help you do anything other than getting out of debt, but bankruptcy can work for you in many other ways if you want it to. Even though your bankruptcy filing remains on your credit report for 7 to 10 years, you can rest assured that you are not going to be marked for life or even for 10 years. In fact, you will find that many companies are willing to work with you to obtain new credit even with a bankruptcy on your credit report.

It is important to note that there will be some barriers to getting back on your feet in the financial sense. Rebuilding your credit takes some effort and strategy on your part, but it is possible. You can turn the bankruptcy filing to your advantage and this section shows you how.

DELETING CREDIT REPORT ERRORS IN 48 HOURS

This is the absolute fastest way to correct mistakes on your credit report and raise your credit score at the same time. However, you can't do this yourself. It can only be done through a mortgage company or a bank. If you apply for a bankruptcy home loan and find errors on your credit report, you can ask the loan officer to conduct a Rapid Rescore. You must be sure not to do this every time you apply for credit, or you can find yourself in bigger problems. The Rapid Rescore strategy takes time because it requires proper paperwork.

You need proof that the item is incorrect. To do this, you need the creditor to admit the account is incorrectly listed on your credit report. For example, you can obtain a letter from the creditor stating that the account is not your account or the account was paid. You can also obtain a release of lien notice, a satisfaction of judgment, a bankruptcy discharge, a letter for deletion of a collection account, or another type of document that substantiates your claim.

The results are not guaranteed, and the cost of the service is about $50 per account, so you should really be wary of taking advantage of it.

DELETING BAD CREDIT

Beware of scam artists offering to eliminate your bad credit. Credit repair clinics charge huge fees for their services and promise you a clean credit report. Sometimes they claim they can give you a new credit profile! People spend hundreds, or even thousands, of dollars for something they can do themselves.

Why? Most people don't realize that they can clean up their credit report without the assistance of a credit report clinic.

Deleting negative credit that is accurate requires help, but removing credit mistakes is much more straightforward. Credit report errors can be corrected by sending a simple dispute letter to the creditor and the credit reporting agency. It's that simple. If you have the paperwork proving the notation is a true error, send copies (not originals) of those documents with the dispute letter to the creditor and send a copy of the letter to the credit reporting agency. Provide a deadline in the letter of 30 days to respond to your request and follow up after the deadline passes.

Even if you don't have documentation to prove a notation is a mistake, you should still send the dispute letter. According to federal law; the credit bureaus have a reasonable amount of time to validate your claim. They will contact the creditor in question for verification of the account. The creditor most provide documentation verifying the account. If the creditor cannot verify the account, the account is deleted or corrected.

The above is a brief explanation of corrected credit report errors. You can find more detailed information from the Federal Trade Commission for disputing errors on credit reports from its website: www.consumer.ftc.gov

RIDE SOMEONE ELSE'S CREDIT COAT TAILS

This is a fast and little-known way to boost your credit score, but it requires a very trusting relationship between you and the person who has the coat tails you will be "riding." A friend or family member adds you to his or her credit account as a joint account holder. By adding you as a joint account holder, the account holder's payment history is now going to be reported on your credit report. If the person has perfect credit, now you will also have excellent credit for that one account. For a larger impact on your credit score, use an aged account. What I mean by this is that if your friend or a family member has a 10-year-old credit card account with a perfect payment history, the length of the credit history also becomes part of your credit file. A long credit history also increases a credit score. This only requires a telephone call from your friend or family member to the credit card company to add you to the account.

If you could secure three to five of these accounts; particularly if they are installment accounts, your credit score could significantly improve very quickly. The hardest part of the process is finding someone who has good credit and who is willing to add you to their account. You already have a low credit score and bad credit, so how eager do you believe someone will be to make you a joint cardholder on the account? Even your parents don't want you to damage their credit by taking on your bad credit.

Here's a way to convince someone to let you ride their good credit coat tails. Tell the person you don't want the credit card and you don't want the credit card information. Without the credit card or information, you are unable to use it to make purchases or at least it makes it much harder for you to do so without the information. Furthermore, most accounts have online access that allows the person to set warnings when a purchase is made with the card. If they set an alert, they know if you use the account for any reason. These steps may entice the person to help you improve your credit rating by allowing you to ride the person's good financial coat tails.

THE ROUND ROBIN PLAN

This strategy is one of the oldest credit building tricks in the books. It used to be accomplished through secured savings accounts, but now it's much easier to do because of the invention of secured credit cards.

Here's how the "Round Robin" works:

- ⬤ Take $1,000 (or whatever you can afford to use) and apply for a secured credit card. Once you receive the card, take a cash advance of 70% of your credit limit.

- ⬤ Apply for a second secured credit card using the funds obtained from the first secured credit card. Once you receive the second secured credit card, take a cash advance of 70% of your credit limit on this card.

- ⬤ Use the money from the cash advance on the second secured credit card to apply for a third secured credit card. Once you receive the third secured credit card, take another cash advance of 70% of your credit limit on this card.

- ⬤ Open a new checking account using the funds from the final cash advance from the third secured credit card. You will only use this account to make payments on your three new credit cards.

If you make your credit card payments on time every month, your credit score will improve because you now have three new perfect payment credit cards. It is important that I point out that at first, your credit score might drop a few points because of the multiple accounts being opened within a short time. However, if you wait for about four months and have no new accounts or any new delinquencies on your report, you will see your credit score begin to increase.

WARNING: I must point out that the round robin can be very risky. If you are not able to leave the money in the account alone, you are taking the risk of making your credit rating much worse. You must make each payment on each card on or before the due date in order for this to work.

PAYMENTS MADE ON OR BEFORE THE DUE DATE

This tip is obvious, but I cannot stress the importance of on-time payments enough. If you don't make each payment on or before the due date, your credit score decreases. The decrease in your credit score occurs regardless of how late your payment is made. A payment that is one day late is just as detrimental to your credit score as a payment that is made one week late. Late payments can harm your credit score quickly and severely as payment history accounts for 35% of your overall credit score.

PAY DOWN YOUR DEBTS

You must remember that you're dealing with high-level statistics and probabilities that evaluate and forecast trends in your financial behavior when looking at your credit rating. You should never pay off your revolving debt entirely because you credit score reflects your ability to manage your credit.

If you pay off your debt, you are not "managing" any debt. If you maintain a balance of nothing, you have nothing to manage. Therefore, when you are thinking in terms of a credit score, you have demonstrated your ability to swiftly pay off accounts so that you can avoid managing them.

Don't get me wrong; if you're overextended to begin with you need to pay off what's necessary to make your credit profile look great. Then you need to manage the remaining credit wisely. Creditors want to know that you can manage your credit account, so you need a few accounts with balances under 30 percent of the credit limit to "balance." Obviously, you want accounts with the lowest interest rates possible because you don't want to pay money you don't have to pay for credit. When your credit score is as high as possible, the need to manage multiple accounts decreases somewhat.

DON'T CLOSE ANY ACCOUNTS

Even if you pay off revolving debts, don't close the account. The longer an account is open with no negative reports on it, the better it reflects in your overall credit score. This occurs because the length that accounts are open are reflected in the calculation of your credit score. If by some chance an old credit account that had a zero balance when you filed bankruptcy is not closed by the creditor, try using that account and paying it off on time. Because it is an older account, you will benefit in two ways — a longer credit history and on-time payments.

DON'T APPLY FOR NEW CREDIT

You should steer away from applying for any new credit unless it is absolutely necessary. Every time you apply for credit, an inquiry is added to your credit report, and every inquiry drops your credit score. This theory doesn't necessarily apply to someone with no to little credit history.

When you have very little to no credit, there is no track record showing how you manage your credit accounts. You must remember, your credit score is about risk assessment. If there is no credit history, there is no way for creditors to assess the risk of lending money to you. To help improve your credit history, apply for credit for your housing, transportation, college, continued education, and a credit card. A good mix of credit used wisely will provide you with a great credit history and excellent credit score.

MIX CREDIT TYPES

If you demonstrate to creditors that you can handle different types of credit at the same time, you are rewarded with a great credit score. To do this, apply for an installment loan, personal loan, or mortgage. Apply for revolving credit with a major credit card company and a retail store. By mixing up your credit accounts, you demonstrate you can manage your credit because you have short term and long term credit accounts with various payment plans and terms. Keep these accounts open with a balance of 70% or less of the credit limit (30 percent is safer if you have a difficult time managing money) and be sure to pay each account on time. As you do this, you will see your credit score improve by leaps and bounds.

DON'T HAVE A BANKRUPTCY OR FORECLOSURE

Here's the most obvious advice: Don't file for bankruptcy relief or have a foreclosure if you can avoid it. These incidents stay on your credit report for 10 years and always decrease your credit score. If you are looking to rebuild your credit history quickly after a bankruptcy or foreclosure, I recommend you use the Round Robin strategy that I mentioned previously using secured credit cards. In time, you will qualify for a car loan and then later a mortgage loan. These loans will continue to help improve your credit score provided you make all payments on or before the due date for each payment. REMEMBER: You can't begin to rebuild your credit until AFTER your bankruptcy case has been closed. You are not permitted to incur new credit during your bankruptcy case without prior court approval.

CHAPTER SEVEN

USING SECURED CREDIT CARDS TO RECOVER FROM BANKRUPTCY – A NECESSARY EVIL

For most of us, the thought of using secured credit cards doesn't seem appealing. However, it is an excellent way to improve your credit rating after a bankruptcy filing. As I stated in the previous section, the round robin strategy is a method of rebuilding your credit using secured credit cards, provided you are careful and dedicated to the strategy.

WHAT IS A SECURED CREDIT CARD?

A secured credit card is just a term used to describe a credit card that you prepay. Your credit limit is equal to the amount of money you place as a deposit with the credit card company. A secured credit card may seem to be no more than paying cash plus interest for goods and services that you could simply pay cash for in the first place.

For this reason, a secured credit card doesn't seem like a good idea at first, but it is a great way to improve your credit score.

Secured credit cards were created for this very reason. As long as you maintain a 70% balance on your credit card and make all payments on time, you will eventually be entitled to an increase in your credit limit. This helps you obtain credit in addition to improving your credit score by reporting on-time payments. In the long run, secured credit cards can help you recover from bankruptcy by improving your credit rating.

EXAMPLES OF SECURED CREDIT CARDS

There are many different types of secured credit cards available right now, and you must be picky about the card you choose. Many banks and companies are offering secured credit cards, so they are competing for your business by offering different incentives. Below are several offers I found for secured credit cards. Since these offers frequently change, you need to read the fine print and check for yourself to ensure you are receiving the benefits and incentives you desire when applying for a secured credit card.

CHASE PREPAID MASTERCARD AND VISA

This prepaid credit card offers 0% interest on your prepaid credit card which is great for helping you to keep the payments current. They require at least a $500-dollar deposit; however, you can pay more. Chase cards are recognized and accepted everywhere that Visa and MasterCard are accepted. Since they also offer unsecured cards, no one will know which version you are using. This is good for the person who really doesn't want it to be obvious they are using a prepaid credit card.

Chase also runs off their own banking institution, so when you have established good standing with them, they may upgrade you to an unsecured credit card by transferring your balance and raising your credit limit. They will usually make a reference to your account after six months. Some other secured credit cards with a similar offer are:

- Orchard Bank Master Cards

- First Bank Visa

- Eufora Prepaid Master Card

- Centennial

- Premier Bank

CAPITAL ONE

The prepaid deal that you will get from Capital One is actually quite remarkable. You can make a deposit and receive a higher credit limit than your deposit amount. This is excellent because they really give you a chance to work on your credit. Capital One does charge fees for cash advances as well as interest fees of up to 25%. That is the big drawback with choosing a Capital one secured credit card. As you are also only allowed to take out 25% of the total limit on cash withdrawals, it makes the round robin approach to rebuilding credit impossible, but it is a great card to have as far as the security deposit and is worth considering.

ONE ADDITIONAL THOUGHT ABOUT SECURED CREDIT CARDS

You can also get rewards cards when you apply for some secured credit cards, so look for that option if earning rewards appeals to you.

You re-establish and improve your credit when you go through any of these or thousands of other offers. I would suggest you try to use banks and financial institutions to obtain your secured credit cards as banks and financial institutions offer better turnaround times for re-establishing your credit. Furthermore, you want to ensure your on-time payments are being reported to the credit reporting agencies. Some companies don't report your payments, but almost all banks and large financial institutions report payments on all accounts, including secured credit cards. Before applying for a secured credit card, read the fine print to ensure the information will be reported to the credit reporting bureaus.

CHAPTER EIGHT

REBUILDING THROUGH A MORTGAGE – NOT AS HARD AS YOU IMAGINE

Many people who go through a bankruptcy or dig themselves out of deep debt promise to themselves to never borrow money again. Credit scores can take a hit when you declare bankruptcy, so it is easy to see why no one wants to go through the process again.

In case you haven't heard, credit scores are the numerical way your credit worthiness is identified to creditors. Your numbers tell creditors what they need to know about you and your financial history.

FICO and VantageScore at two types of scores lenders can look at when determining your credit rating. The numbers below may fluctuate between agencies, but it will give you a good general rule of thumb.
How does your credit rank?

☺   750 and higher – Excellent

☺ 700 to 749 – Good credit
😐 650 to 699 – Fair credit
☹ 600 to 649 – Poor credit
☹ Below 600 – Bad credit

Don't be discouraged if you did not get a "happy face" because the information in this book is designed to help you turn that frown upside down!

Another important note that you should understand is that credit scores are not just used for borrowing money. Credit scores impact just about every aspect of your financial life. Examples of companies or entities that use credit scores to decide whether to do business with you AND potentially set your payment rates with those companies include:

➲ Potential Employers

➲ Auto, Life, and Health Insurance Companies

➲ Apartment Rental and Other Rental Companies

➲ Banks (for opening bank accounts)

➲ Some Utility Companies

If your credit score is having a negative impact on your life, you may want to consider using a mortgage to improve your credit score. A mortgage may sound ridiculous because it is a major debt but a mortgage is a

great way to prove your credit worthiness to other companies. A mortgage is the quickest, easiest, safest, and best way to rebuild your scores. Let me show you how.

✓ Quick – You can't do anything that will move your credit scores higher faster than a mortgage. The reason for this is because it is a larger debt and carries a lot of weight in your scores because of it.

✓ Simple - Believe it or not, getting a decent mortgage is much easier than getting a decent credit card or car loan. Pre-approval is a great way to go about it.

✓ Safe - You are already paying rent for your house or apartment, so why not pay to own? It is a debt that you must pay anyway, so why not make it work for you?

✓ Makes Sense - Mortgage lenders are considered by your scores as a bank loan. They are not third rate lenders like the credit card, auto loans, personal loans that are always available to you. Third Rate Lenders have an adverse effect on scores, but mortgages are looked at as a real asset and getting one is a sure-fire way to improve your score.

TIPS TO REFINANCING YOUR MORTGAGE

Deciding If a Mortgage Refinance Is Your Best Option

When you are ready to use mortgage refinancing as a way to achieve a "happy face" credit score after a bankruptcy, it can be hard to know if refinancing a mortgage is the best choice for you now. Refinancing a mortgage after a bankruptcy can also be scary. You just got a fresh start so why mess that up? For some people, a mortgage refinance offers great financial benefits, but for others, it may never be worth it. Ask yourself these questions to help determine if a mortgage refinance is a good option for you right now:

- How long do you plan to be in the house? Is it long enough to make refinancing the home worth the cost of a refinance?

- How much higher will the interest rate be on your new loan taking into consideration your poor credit score?

- If you are not paying private mortgage insurance on your current mortgage, will refinancing the mortgage result in this added expense each month?

- How much are the closing costs for the new loan?

- Are there any extra fees and charges that will make the loan less affordable to pay back?

- Do you have sufficient equity to make an equity line a more affordable and sensible option?

- Can you really afford it?

If you are wondering whether mortgage refinancing is a good idea after bankruptcy, it is a great way to improve your credit score at a faster speed. Of course, you must consider your answers to the above questions. Here are a few general mortgage refinancing tips that may help to make the process easier for you or help you make your decisions if you are on the fence about a mortgage refinance:

- If you don't plan to stay in the house very long, refinancing may not be the right option for you at this time.

- Unless you qualify for an interest rate that you can afford, refinancing your home may cost you more money than you can really afford to pay. It will also cost you thousands of dollars more in the long run compared to waiting until your credit is a bit better and you qualify for a lower interest rate.

- Keep an eye on interest rates, especially variable interest rates that change frequently. If your credit is too poor, you may not qualify for a fixed interest rate. If so, you must know when the interest rate can change and by how much. For example, an interest rate that is locked into changing only one time per year and is capped at no more than one percentage point in change may not be too risky, but these are usually on mortgages. Second mortgages may carry a variable interest rate that is based on the prime plus "a number" and can change as often as every quarter with no cap. This type of variable rate could become very costly.

- Only refinance your mortgage if it benefits you beyond improving your credit score. If you get in over your head, you will just end up back in bankruptcy or worse. Improving your credit score is not a sufficient reason alone to enter into a new mortgage.

🏠 If you are paying private mortgage insurance on your current mortgage, refinancing might help you to get rid of this extra expense.

CHOOSING A LENDER FOR A MORTGAGE REFINANCE

When you want to take advantage of mortgage refinancing to improve your financial situation, the most important decisions you make involve interest rates and the lender you choose for your new mortgage.

A prior bankruptcy filing can create more costs when you decide to refinance your mortgage. Closing costs can be higher, and interest rates will definitely be higher. Interest rates are high for bad credit borrowers. The amount of interest you pay significantly impacts your monthly mortgage payment and the total amount of money you pay over the life of the loan. The lower your interest rate, the better off you will be down the road.

The lender you choose can have a huge impact on your mortgage refinance. By using a lender who offers low-interest rates, low lending fees, and decreased closing costs, you can save lots of money and indeed make your efforts to refinance worthwhile. However, it may be difficult to find the right lender with a bankruptcy on your credit history. A few tips I can offer to help you in your search for a mortgage lender include:

1. When you are refinancing after a bankruptcy, don't take the first offer that comes around. Take some time and research your choices. Make comparisons and seek reviews from borrowers like you.

2. When you have bad credit, you need to find a lender who is willing to work with you and offer you reasonable loan terms. There are lenders out there who work with individuals with poor credit. You can find a good one, but again, it takes time and work.

3. Know your credit score before you begin looking for a mortgage lender. Knowing your score is beneficial to you. Try to get rid of as many blemishes on your credit report as you can before applying for a refinance. Even though you have a bankruptcy on your credit report, you may still qualify for a good loan but only if you have cleared any mistakes on your report before you began the process of finding a mortgage company.

CHAPTER NINE

USING HOME EQUITY TO REGAIN CREDIT — GETTING SOME LEVERAGE

If you have recently been through bankruptcy, it can be difficult to find money that you need for an emergency, to make repairs, pay for college, or pay for another need. The fact is that regardless of how hard you try, it might seem that your bankruptcy is always standing in your way; at least for the next 7 to 10 years. If this happens to you, you might consider a home equity loan to help rebuild your credit and obtain the money you need. There are several advantages of using a home equity loan to cover your financial needs, but it may be difficult to find a lender who will agree to loan you the money at a reasonable interest rate.

First of all, when you're looking at a home equity loan, it's important you understand exactly what equity is before you use it. Equity is the difference between the fair market value of your home less any liens against your home. For example, if your home is worth $100,000 and you owe $60,000 on your mortgage, your equity is $40,000. The more equity that is in your home, the more value you have to request a home equity loan.

When you are seeking a home equity loan, the equity you have built up in your home is a valuable asset. The higher the equity in your home, the better interest rate you may qualify for with a bank. If you have $40,000 in equity and you are requesting a $20,000 line of credit, the bank knows that it is fully protected by the lien it places on the home should you default on the loan. However, this is not the case for all banks. You should shop around to find a bank that offers the lowest interest rate on home equity loans BEFORE you apply for the loan. You don't want to apply with numerous banks because each application will "ding" your credit report lowering your credit rating.

Beware of Pitfalls Associated with Home Equity Loans

The fact is that you can get credit again after bankruptcy. Bankruptcy is meant to give you a fresh financial start, and the ability to rebuild credit is part of that new start. Of course, like all good things; there is a process you must follow to rebuild credit after bankruptcy, and it can be full of pitfalls. Some of these pitfalls can be avoided.

Don't take out loans or use credit unless you can afford to make the payments on time.

This may sound obvious, but many good consumers make the mistake of taking out loans they can't afford to pay. Don't get so eager to rebuild your credit after bankruptcy that you feel you need to rush into it. You need to figure out whether you can afford the payments. If you assume you can keep the payments every month but can afford to miss a few after a while, you will never rebuild your credit and will likely end up back in debt. You're going to need detailed information to take out a new loan in order to ensure you have the income to pay all payments.

Check your budget.

If you don't have a budget; create one before you even consider applying for new credit. With your budget, figure out exactly how much you can afford to pay for a new loan. Then use a loan calculator to calculate the amount of the new loan payment. Compare the amount of the payment to your available income. Available income means reliable income that is not committed to another area of your budget. Don't base it on money you might have, work with the money you do have right now. Don't forget to leave some room for savings and emergencies in your budget. If you cannot fit the new payment into your budget leaving room for emergencies and savings, you can't afford the new payment.

Beware of hidden fees.

Many reputable lenders specialize in offering second chance loans, but they have a higher interest rate. These types of loans are offered to consumers who have low credit scores or have filed bankruptcy. Not all lenders who offer these loans are reputable. When you've filed bankruptcy and know your credit options are limited, you may be tempted to accept terms that would usually sound ridiculous. Lenders know this fact, and some take advantage of post-bankruptcy clients by adding unnecessary fees, crippling late-payment charges, and hidden costs. Beware of lenders who benefit from customers who are desperate for a loan.

You need to ask for a list of the fees and costs associated with the new loan. Don't be lulled into a false sense of security by terms like, "No up-front costs." Many credit cards that target post-bankruptcy and low-scoring consumers add "processing charges" and "annual fees" directly to your account—which means that you may receive a credit card with a $250 credit limit and $175 or more in charges already made to the account. Watch for similar tactics on home equity loans.

Know the penalties for late payments and going over your credit limit.

Often, one late payment can send an account spiraling out of control. If you miss one payment and a $35 late charge is added, the late fee could push you over the limit if you withdrew the full amount of the loan and had not yet paid the principal amount of the loan down. The late charge puts you over your credit limit triggering another $35 charge, which puts you further over your credit limit. By the time your next statement comes in the mail, your minimum payment has turned into a request for $450 or more to "bring your account current." If you aren't able to make that payment, the past due portion continues to grow larger. For many post-bankruptcy consumers, this scenario is all too familiar. There's no room for this kind of error when you're trying to rebuild after bankruptcy, so be very certain you know what kind of charges may apply and what circumstances might trigger them.

Read the entire agreement carefully.

It's true that most people don't read the fine print in their contracts, but it's a gamble, and it's all the more dangerous when you're dealing with high-risk lenders. Remember that companies making loans to low-credit-scoring and post-bankruptcy consumers are taking a chance—and they're not going to take the risk without a significant payoff. Read and understand the entire agreement. If you don't understand something, ask questions until you do understand it.

Watch Out for Common "Predatory" Practices

People who have filed for bankruptcy are often targeted by predatory lenders. These lenders know that post-bankruptcy borrowers have fewer options and they may be so relieved to discover they've qualified for a loan after bankruptcy that they won't be inclined to ask too many questions. Many consumers accept these practices because they think accepting extortionist terms is the only way that they'll qualify for credit after bankruptcy. It's not true. Hold out for a reputable post-bankruptcy lender.

You should also watch out for predatory lenders who try to get you with the bait and switch method. A lender reels you in by promising you one set of terms and then changes the terms on you after you have agreed to the contract. For example, a contract that has a variable interest rate that can be changed at any time. Be aware of this trick and look for it.

Another common method is called loan packing. This is when your lender insists or even demands you add a bunch of other services to your loan, such as insurance or credit protection. These add-ons are not forcible, and if a lender tries to tell you it is, the lender is lying. Take your business elsewhere.

Loan flipping is another tactic lenders use with post-bankruptcy borrowers. They try to get you to repeatedly refinance your home equity loan. This process strips your home's equity. The lender can even charge you more fees for doing it, so beware. Only take out loans that you want and nothing else. Don't let a lender try to change your mind.

The fresh start you gained in bankruptcy can be exactly what you need to get your financial life back on track and establish strong credit. Don't let dishonest and unethical lenders, or your over-eagerness, push you to do something you are not comfortable with. Remember to read the fine print in all written documentation, ask questions, and don't be afraid to walk out without signing anything if you feel uncomfortable or unsure.

Finding an Equity Lender

Finding a lender for a post-bankruptcy home equity loan often requires you to take a little time to shop around and compare quotes before you can find one you are comfortable using. Searching online can help you make comparisons but be careful that you are not giving the company authority to run your credit. You should not authorize a credit check until you have chosen a lender and you are ready to complete a loan application. Online lenders are often consulted for equity loans since they can usually offer a lower interest rate than many walk-in lenders. However, it's important that you take the time to compare different loan offers and choose the one that's best for you and your needs. Not all lenders are the same — some lenders are better than others. In addition to comparing offers, check the lender's reputation before signing up.

It is worth pointing out that with so many prime lenders to choose from, it is easy to become overwhelmed trying to find one. It is imperative that you base your loan search solely on the money that you have available to repay a loan. You should also only work with lenders who offer no-obligation loan quotes to compare rates and fees.

With most home equity loans, you may see fees such as annual processing fees or minimum balance fees. These fees are more likely to be a part of the terms of the loan rather than upfront fees. Since these fees can add hundreds of dollars to your loan costs, it is very important that you check the fine print extremely carefully when applying for a home equity loan.

After you have chosen your lender, the application process is simple. As a matter of fact, some lenders allow you to apply online, and you can get an answer within minutes or days. A home equity loan can be an easy way to help you rebuild your credit after bankruptcy. However, I can't stress enough that you ONLY apply for a home equity loan if you KNOW you can afford the payment AFTER preparing a budget.

CHAPTER TEN

CREDIT REPAIR COMPANIES – DO YOUR DUE DILIGENCE

If you have filed a bankruptcy case, you can't get credit for ten years.

This is a typical lie that credit repair companies tell you, so you will hire them to help you get credit. The truth is you can start building a positive credit history as soon as your bankruptcy case is closed and discharged. While creditors will be cautious in dealing with you at first, you can slowly show your fiscal responsibility and build a solid history that will lead lenders to view you as a good credit risk long before the bankruptcy is off your history report.

WARNING SIGNS OF A BAD CREDIT REPAIR COMPANY

As much as we want to believe that credit repair companies want to help out the underdog, many of the companies are unscrupulous and are only out to make a dollar. They lie and charge ridiculous fees and even commit outright fraud in their pursuit of profit. Fortunately, there are warning signs that you can see beforehand to recognize bad credit repair companies.

- ☒ Don't use a credit repair company that doesn't follow industry standards or regulations to the letter. To find out about industry standards or regulations, go to your own state government website and check.

- ☒ Don't use a credit repair company that claims to be able to wipe out or get rid of your bankruptcy altogether; to remove accurate negative information from your credit history, or claim to be able to obtain credit for you no matter what your credit history states.

- ☒ Don't use a credit repair company that promises to utilize some sort of secret or little-known holes in the system as a way to help you to remove information from your credit history.

- ☒ Don't use a credit repair company unless it easily gives you a written disclosure of your rights in relation to your credit history before they ask you to sign a contract. Any contract that you sign has to include all the terms and conditions of payment, a thoroughly detailed description of the services they are providing to you, including any guarantees of performance, and an estimate of how long it will take for the contract to be completed. The agreement should also include a right to cancel the contract for at least three days, in case you have second thoughts.

☒ Don't use a credit repair company that tries to charge money before it has actually done anything to fix your credit.

☒ Don't use a credit repair company that tries to keep you from directly contacting the major credit bureaus on your own.

CHAPTER ELEVEN

COMMON CREDIT REPAIR SCAMS – THE DARK SIDE OF BANKRUPTCY

With so many people looking for credit help after they have filed a bankruptcy petition, many people are willing to capitalize off the bad luck of a bankruptcy debtor. You can find thousands of different advertisements online and elsewhere that promise you credit repair. Not all of these claims are legal. In this section, I address the most common credit report scams so you can be armed with information to help you avoid these scams.

Let's look at them now!

SCAM #1 – Getting A New Social Security Number

You are only allowed to have one Social Security number. It's against the law to use a different Social Security number to create a false identity. However, many criminals offer this service to you for a fee. It is illegal, and you would be in for quite a bit of trouble. Not to mention, nobody ever seems to wonder just where these SSNs come from. It is most likely that you are paying for a stolen identity. It is a perfect scam for the thief because you are the person who will be arrested for identity theft. It is quite brilliant, and many people fall for it. Even if they claim that this transaction is entirely legal; IT IS NOT!!!!

SCAM #2 - Getting A Federal Employer Identification Number

A Federal Employer Identification Number can be abbreviated as EIN or FEIN. This number is nothing more than a file segregation scam. For this scam, the criminal claims you can obtain a federal tax ID number, as if you are a business, and end up with a clean credit record under that tax ID number. It is against the law to use an EIN to set up a false identity. Let me also tell you that a new credit report under an EIN will not show a credit history. It is unlikely that a creditor would regard a new business with no credit history as a good credit risk. So, it is also a waste of time.

SCAM #3 - Challenging Everything Bad on A Credit Report

As I stated before, this is simply a waste of your time. All credit agencies must keep accurate records of negative entries on your credit history, including bankruptcy filings, for seven to 10 years. Sometimes accurate negative information may be reported beyond those time periods, but it is rare. You can't report false negatives on your credit report without suffering some consequences. If you are caught filing false claims, you can face serious penalties.

SCAM #4 - Clean Credit Scam

Scam artists claim they clean your credit fast and use their contacts to obtain a mortgage, car loan, or credit card account for you. This is one of the more recent credit repair scams, and coincidentally it is also one of the most expensive. Con artists dangle the promise of needed money or loans in front of the desperate consumer as an incentive for the consumer to pay them up-front fees that never seem to end.

Scammers may imitate actual banks or financial institutions in their effort to appear legitimate. Since there are genuine nonprofit groups who do help teach consumers and assist them in finding affordable mortgage loans, scammers may also try to imitate these companies. Any reputable community-based organizations tend to focus more on education, and they don't charge expensive, never-ending fees for their services. True, legitimate non-profit companies work with lenders and government agencies you should have already heard of, and are able to prove it.

SCAM #5 - The 900-Number for Details on How to Fix Your Credit

This is a pitiful scam, but it is still effective and is often combined with many of the other scams mentioned above. While you are looking for help, the con artists are looking for ways to keep you on the line as long as possible because you are being charged by the minute for the telephone call. It's just like every other 900 number scam. Scammers are often vague on details when they are talking to you on the phone. If you have trouble defining, understanding, or explaining their proposed plan for cleaning your credit, that is a clue you are being scammed.

You should also watch out for any offer of guaranteed credit with these 900 numbers as it is almost certainly a fraud. This is the same with anyone who claims quick fixes. You should really be on the lookout for nameless, faceless so called credit repair companies.

ASK QUESTIONS AND DEMAND ANSWERS

Legitimate counselors want a face-to-face meeting to go over your financial details with you, and they also spend lots of time trying to educate you on the process. Below are some important questions you need to ask if you want to be sure you are not dealing with a scammer:

? Who is coming up with the plan, and who can I speak to about it?

? Has this company had any problems before? You can find out by calling your state's regulatory or consumer offices to see if there are any complaints or any actions being taken against the company. Don't forget to check with the company's home state if you have to, and to run the business and names of the company's chief executives through a couple of search engines.

? How are they paid, how much are they paid, and when do they receive their payment? Since you can do your own credit repair for free, this is why you should ask. It may be more beneficial to do it yourself. You should choose an organization that is affiliated with the two main nonprofits, the National Foundation for Credit Counseling and the Association of Independent Consumer Credit Counseling Agencies. They will help you for a small fee that is nowhere near the hundreds of dollars a scammer charges.

? What's the downside of this plan, if any? An experienced credit counselor is careful to present the positives and negatives behind any plan. When a person is scamming you, he ignores the bad side and focuses on the upside.

? Did you contact them or did they contact you?

? Why aren't you doing it for yourself?

I should also note that you should not be told to make payments for your credit report. You're entitled to receive a free copy of each of your credit reports every 12 months. If you have not requested a copy of your credit reports within the past 12 months, you can do so for free at AnnualCreditReport.com. Watch out for sites and services that are trying to charge you for credit reports or that are trying to charge you for your credit report when you opt for their credit monitoring service.

CHAPTER TWELVE

ERASING CREDIT DAMAGE: A STEP BY STEP PROCESS

Basically, you can't wipe out the past. Negative records, such as bankruptcies, foreclosures, repossessions, and collection accounts remain on your credit report for 7 to 10 years. There is nothing you can do to speed up the time it takes for these notations to fall off your credit report. However; with some time and effort, you can improve your credit rating even before the negative notations expire. Below are five easy steps you can take to rebuild your credit before your bankruptcy filing is removed from your credit history.

Step 1: Check Out the Damage

The first step in rebuilding your credit is to find out where your credit stands right now. This is an important step to take, which is why I have discussed it more than once in this book. Your report can change every week, so checking it often is necessary. You can easily obtain your credit report online or by writing to the credit reporting agencies. Checking your own credit data never damages your credit scores — that is a myth.

Print each report and review it very carefully. Highlight any negative records or errors that are damaging your credit score. You must understand what your credit report says because if you don't understand what is contained in your credit report, how can you expect to correct it? Most reports contain an explanation of the terms used in the report. If you require more information, visit the website for the credit reporting agency. Most companies have a Q&A on their website or a special section on "How to read your credit report" to help you understand the various sections and terms in your credit report.

Step 2: Check the Expiration Dates

By law, negative records remain on your credit report for 7 to 10 years. The exact expiration date will vary; depending upon the type of record. Paying off an old collection debt or discharging your bankruptcy does not get rid of these records; contrary to what most people believe. The record is only noted as "paid" or "included in bankruptcy."

For each of the negative records you see on your credit report (including judgments, liens, charge-offs, late payments, bankruptcy filings, and collection records), you can look up the exact date that each account is set to fall off your credit report. It is good to know when accounts will fall off your record so you know when you can expect to see a major improvement in your credit score.

Step 3: Dispute the Errors

I can't stress this step enough! Can you tell by how many times I refer to correcting errors on credit reports in this book?

If you find anything at all that appears to be incorrect, such as fraudulent accounts or records that should have expired, on your credit reports, you have the right to dispute these errors. To do this, you need to send a separate dispute letter to the creditor and each of the three credit bureaus (Equifax, Experian, and TransUnion). Once your dispute is received, the credit bureaus have 30 days to investigate your dispute and determine whether or not to make the change you requested.

Don't try to dispute information that is accurate. Accurate information cannot be removed from your credit reports, and it is a waste of time to attempt to dispute these records because it will not help you. Just because you don't believe an account is fair doesn't mean that you need to dispute the record. If you owed the debt, even if you disagreed with the debt, you still owe the debt. You must have a legal reason for disputing a debt. In addition, disputing positive information may harm your credit scores and cause you to garner fraud charges.

Step 4: Keep Track of The Positive

Just like the need to remove or correct inaccuracies, you should also report anything positive that is not included in your credit report. Since there is no way to remove negative information from your credit report, the best way to improve your score is to add as much new positive information as you can.

You can begin with the round robin approach I discussed in a previous section. However, your efforts shouldn't stop there. You should also sign up for an online banking service that allows you keep a close eye on your accounts. If you see a discrepancy, you can easily print the information to file with your dispute. Online banking is a great way to keep on top of information. You can also use online banking to make instant payments to creditors by adding them to your automatic payment plans. This ensures all your payments are made on time.

Step 5: Monitor Your Progress

It's easy to keep track of your credit score improvement because we now have a great deal of software that can do it for you. Instead of just giving you random access to your credit report and general email alerts, these new credit monitoring programs give you access to your credit reports and credit scores, identity theft and fraud protection, credit score monitoring, daily alerts, and more. You can also register with an online credit monitoring service that sends you information by email every day.

Once you register with a credit monitoring service, you can track your credit score progress closely. Your credit score should regularly improve as you continue to use your credit responsibly and add new positive information to your credit reports.

CHAPTER THIRTEEN

CREDIT MONITORING SERVICES – KNOWLEDGE IS POWER

To be able to use a credit monitoring service to its full potential, it helps if you fully understand how these services work and how they can benefit you. Credit report monitoring can be used after bankruptcy to help you as part of an identity theft prevention and detection strategy. Although monitoring your credit report may not prevent many of the credit problems that we often find ourselves in, these services can keep you up to date with anything that is going awry.

After you file for bankruptcy relief, you want to know exactly what is going on with your credit report. There are a variety of reasons why a credit monitoring service is the best way for you to keep records of your credit report and scoring information. In the era of online identity fraud, you need this type of protection more than ever. Nothing will undermine your efforts to recover from bankruptcy faster than having your identity stolen. This section of the book focuses on the things you should know about credit monitoring services so that if you are considering using one, you can make an informed choice.

Some companies make their advertisements sound as if the company monitors your credit report so that at the precise moment an identity thief is at work, alarms are sounded, the thief is stopped, and you are fully aware of the theft. Although this is truly why these services exist, the way that they really work is not as spectacular. The general purpose of credit monitoring services can really be explained in these basic points:

Early Activity Detection: The basic benefit and purpose of credit monitoring services are that they help you quickly detect any unauthorized activity that takes place in your name. As I stated earlier, the victims often have 6 months of activity recorded in their name before they even know about it. Therefore, early detection can save you thousands of dollars and a lot of headaches, frustration, and anger.

It is Convenient: Most of the services that a credit monitoring service provides can actually be performed by you. However, hiring a monitoring service to do the work for you frees up much of your time. Because these companies have experience handling these matters, the information provided is extremely accurate. It could take you a long time to learn the ins and outs of creditor monitoring, therefore, your information may not be as accurate for a long time.

What Types of Information Do Credit Monitoring Services Monitor?

Although you can pay for many different levels of service, most plans monitor for these things:

☑ Credit File Inquiries. The service keeps track of who is filing inquiries on your credit file and why. This information can be useful in detecting unauthorized activities.

☑ New Account Activity. The service monitors new accounts that are opened in your name and reports it to you.

☑ Address Changes. You can use the service to ensure that no one changes your address, which happens when identity thieves are applying for credit so that they can get credit cards and bills sent to them at another address.

☑ Collection Accounts. Unfortunately, many victims realize their identity has been stolen when they apply for and can't get credit because of multiple collection accounts. Your monitoring service alerts you whenever a collection account is added to your credit file.

☑ Changes to Account Information. The service monitors any changes to account information and informs you of the changes.

☑ Credit Limit Increases. When a peson steals your identification, he increases your credit limits to take advantage of the additional credit that is available. You are notified of any credit limit requests.

☑ Changes to Public Records. The service monitors changes to public records that could indicate identity theft, such as bankruptcy filings, lawsuits, and other public documents that are filed in your name.

☑ Changes to All Existing Accounts. You are notified if your accounts become delinquent.

☑ Account Closures. Any accounts that are closed are flagged and reported to you.

Now that you know what the credit monitoring services actually monitor, you need to know what to look for in a monitoring service. When researching credit monitoring services, look for:

Source. The monitoring service has to use a credit reporting agency to monitor your credit report. However, depending on the service, the information may be obtained from just one or all three major reporting agencies. For this reason, you want to purchase a service or plan that monitors all three credit reporting agencies.

Frequency. When searching for a monitoring service, consider how often they check information. Services vary and provide daily, weekly, or monthly monitoring. You want daily or weekly monitoring of your accounts.

Credit Updates. Some services also provide periodic credit updates. This is different from the alerts because alerts only deal in changes. A periodic credit update adds the information in your credit accounts that have not changed to your report from the monitoring company.

Credit Reports. Monitoring programs offer you a copy of your credit report. How often you receive copies vary depending on the service. Some services provide unlimited access to your credit file which means that you can check it whenever you want to check your report. Other services provide a credit report on a quarterly basis. I would suggest that you sign up for a service that offers you unlimited access to your credit reports because having a current credit report is helpful when you are trying to recover and rebuild after bankruptcy.

Identity Theft Insurance. Some services offer identity theft insurance as part of the package. Just be sure to read the fine print to understand what the insurance covers and the limits of the insurance offered.

Cost. Cost is obviously something you must consider when choosing a monitoring service. Prices range from $39 per year for a very basic, one bureau monitoring service to $200 per year for a premium 3-bureau monitoring service.

When you are working to recover from bankruptcy, keeping track of all your credit accounts is essential to keep you on track. Of course, there may be some things that a credit monitoring service doesn't do for you, but it does provide you with a wealth of information so you can take whatever steps necessary to protect yourself and improve your financial well-being. Preventing identity theft is necessary for recovering from bankruptcy because it can save you from unauthorized attempts made on your account that could put you right back where you started.

CHAPTER FOURTEEN

PREVENTING IDENTITY THEFT – DON'T LET YOUR HARD WORK GO TO WASTE

A credit monitoring service can help with this, but it can't do everything for you. Other things can assist you in your fight to protect your identity. When you declare bankruptcy, you do it to get a second chance. This can't happen if your identity is stolen from you. This section of the book is an expanded discussion of ways you can protect your identity.

The crime of identity theft is on the rise in this country. Recent surveys show there are currently approximately nine million victims of identity theft each year. Criminals steal Social Security numbers, driver's licenses, credit card numbers, ATM cards, calling cards, and anything else they can get their hands on that provides your information. Some criminals go through your garbage or steal your mail to get information. They use the information they gather to impersonate their victims, spending as much money as they can in as short a time as possible before moving on to someone else.

Right now, there are two basic types of identity theft:

➲ **Account Takeover:** Account takeover occurs when a thief obtains your current credit account information and purchases products and services using the actual credit card or by using the account number, expiration date, and code on the back of the card.

➲ **Application Fraud:** Application fraud is also called "true name fraud." The thief uses your SSN and other identification information to open new accounts in your name. It takes a much longer amount of time to find out about this type of fraud unless you have a credit monitoring system working for you.

Generally, victims of credit card fraud are not liable for more than the first $50 of the loss (Lending Act, Fair Credit Billing Act, 15 U. S. C. §1601) provided they report the loss within a certain period of time. Most of the time, the victim isn't required to pay any part of the loss. However, debit card users have less protection against fraud. When this type of fraud occurs, your accounts are wiped out, but you could be liable for the total amount of the loss depending on how quickly it is reported (Electronic Funds Transfer Act, 15 U. S. C. §1693).

Even though most victims are not stuck paying their imposters' bills, victims are often left with a bad credit report that can be even worse when you are trying to recover from a bankruptcy filing. Meanwhile, the victim finds it difficult to obtain credit, new loans, rent an apartment and even get hired for a new job. You can't take advantage of any of these efforts to help you learn to rebuild your credit when you are the victim of fraud. Do you see now why this section is so important?

How Do Thieves Get Personal Information?

Victims of identity theft find that the police can't do much to help, as it can be hard to prove that the fraud took place. Stealing wallets was once the best way identity thieves had to obtain Social Security numbers, driver's licenses, credit card numbers, and other pieces of identification. You report your wallet stolen to law enforcement and maybe they can retrieve it or identify who took your wallet through surveillance cameras or other evidence.

Today, thieves have ways of obtaining your information without you knowing about it at all. Here is how:

- "Dumpster diving" in trash bins is common. Criminals look for unshredded credit card and loan applications or other documents that contain Social Security numbers.

- Stealing mail from mailboxes can give thieves access to brand new credit cards, bank and credit card statements, pre-approved credit offers, investment reports, insurance statements, and even tax information.

- Accessing your credit report is easy if the thief is an employer, loan officer, or landlord.

- Thieves obtain names and SSNs from personnel or customer files in the workplace.

- Shoulder snatching at ATM machines and direct debit purchase sites is an easy way to obtain pin numbers.

- Internet sources, such as public record sites and fee-based information broker sites.

- Sending emails from banks asking you to visit a website that looks like the bank website in order to confirm account information. This type of fraud is known as phishing, and it becomes more popular every day.

You can't prevent identity theft in every case as identity theft is relatively easy because of lax credit industry practices, careless information-handling practices in the workplace, and the simplicity that goes with obtaining someone's Social Security number. But you can reduce your risk of fraud by following the tips in this section.

Tips for Avoiding Identity Theft

The most important advice I can give you is to check your credit report at least once a year. You can catch fraud quicker this way if you don't have a creditor monitoring service in place. Below are more tips you can use to prevent a thief from stealing your identity.

1. Decrease the number of credit and debit cards you carry in your wallet. I recommend against the use of debit cards because of the potential for shoulder snatching. Instead, only carry one or two credit cards in your wallet. Take advantage of online access to your bank account to monitor account activity on a daily basis. Report any strange activity immediately to your bank to decrease your liability.

2. When you are using your credit and debit cards at restaurants and stores, pay close attention to how the magnetic stripe information is taken. Dishonest employees have been known to use a small handheld device that are called skimmers to quickly swipe the card, and then they download the account number data onto a personal computer for use later.

3. Don't use debit cards when you are shopping online. Use a credit card because you are better protected in case of fraud.

4. Photocopy all your credit cards, debit cards, bank accounts, and other financial information, such as the account numbers and expiration dates. Just don't carry the copies with you in your wallet or purse. This way if the information is stolen, you can report it quickly to the correct companies.

5. Never give out your SSN, credit or debit card number, or other personal information over the phone, by mail, or on the Internet, even if you are the one that initiated the contact.

6. Always take credit card receipts with you whenever you get one. Never toss the receipts in a public trash container. Also, don't carry receipts in the shopping bag.

7. Never allow your credit card number to be written onto your checks.

8. Watch the mail when you expect a new credit card to arrive. If your mail has been stolen, consider a post office box.

9. Get a free credit report from Equifax, TransUnion, and Experian once a year at AnnualCreditReport.com.

10. If your state allows the practice, freeze your credit reports. By freezing your credit reports, you can prevent credit issuers from accessing your credit files except when you give your express permission. In most states, security freezes are available for free.

11. Several companies offer credit monitoring services for an annual fee ranging from $40-$200 a year. I advise you take advantage of this service.

12. There are many identity theft insurance products that you can use. I don't recommend them unless they are free or a cheap add-on to an existing insurance policy.

13. When you are dealing with passwords and PINs, don't use the last four digits of your Social Security number, birth date, middle name, consecutive numbers, or anything else that could easily be discovered by thieves. You should use passwords that combine both letters, numbers, and characters.

14. Ask your financial institutions to add extra security protection to your account. Most banks allow you use more than one security feature when accessing your account. Again, don't use passwords that are easy to figure out. If you are asked to create a reminder question, don't use a question that is easily answered by anyone who knows your personal information.

15. Memorize all passwords. Don't write them down. If you can't remember your passwords, use a secure password service such as Last Pass or Dashlane to maintain your passwords.

16. Cover your hand when you use an ATM machine or debit machine.

17. Protect your Social Security number at all costs. Only give it out when it is absolutely necessary. It is this information that the thieves are looking for when they want to steal an identity. If a business asks you for your SSN, you should ask if there is an alternative number that can be used instead. Ask to see the company's written policy on SSNs.

18. Don't have your SSN or driver's license number placed on your checks. This may sound like a given, but you would be surprised how many people do this.

19. Don't say your SSN out loud in public. Don't let anyone say it out loud either.

20. Examine your Social Security Personal Earnings and Benefits Estimate Statement each year.

21. Don't carry your Social Security card in your wallet unless you know you will need it.

22. If you live in a state that uses your SSN as your driver's license number, ask for a different number.

23. Use a firewall on your home computer that helps keep hackers from obtaining your personal identifying information and financial data from your hard drive. This is especially important if you are using DSL or a cable modem.

24. Install and update virus protection software to prevent a worm or virus from obtaining your information.

25. Password-protect your files that contain personal information, such as banking information and credit card information.

26. When shopping online, do business with companies that provide transaction security protection such as Verisign and read their privacy policies.

27. Before you get rid of your computer, use a wipe-out utility program. Deleting information is just not sufficient to protect your identity.

28. Never respond to email messages asking for your personal information, no matter who they are from. Your bank won't ask for personal information by email. They will call or send a written letter requesting you contact the bank.

29. Be aware of file-sharing and file-swapping programs like Ares, eMule, and Vuze.

30. Never carry extra credit cards, debit cards, your Social Security card, birth certificate, or passport in your wallet or purse.

31. If possible, don't carry other cards in your wallet that contain your Social Security number, except on days when you need them.

32. If you want to lower the amount of personal information that is in cyberspace you can do these things:

- Take your name off the marketing lists of the three credit reporting bureaus;

- Sign up for the Federal Trade Commission's National Don't Call Registry;

- Sign up for the Direct Marketing Association's Mail Preference Service;

- Have your name and address removed from the

phone book and reverse directories.

33. Install a mailbox you can lock at your house, use a post office box, or a commercial mailbox service.

34. When you are ordering new checks, pick them up at the bank. Don't have checks mailed to your home.

35. When you pay bills, never leave the envelopes that have your checks or money orders in at your mailbox for the postal carrier to pick up. Take those items to the post office to mail.

36. Each month, review your credit card, bank, and phone statements carefully for any strange items.

37. Try to make as many of your bill payments through automatic deductions from your checking account or use internet banking and pay them yourself.

38. Don't throw out pre-approved credit offers without tearing them up or shredding them.

39. Use a gel pen to write your checks because it has been stated that gel ink contains tiny particles of color that are trapped in the paper, so it is tough to wash the check and re-write it.

40. You must demand that financial institutions keep your data safe. Don't let your bank use easy to decode numbers on your cards. If you have been given the last four digits of your Social Security number as a default PIN, change it to something else immediately. Insist your bank destroys paper and magnetic records before disposing of them.

41. When you complete loan or credit applications, ask

how the company disposes of the paper applications. Some auto dealerships, department stores, car rental agencies, and other companies have been known to be careless with customer applications once they are finished processing the applications. When you pay by credit card, ask the business how it stores and disposes of the receipts. When you transact business online, be sure the company uses secure transmission and storage methods.

42. Store all canceled checks in a safe place. If you rent a storage locker, take extra precautions when you store canceled checks, tax returns, and other sensitive financial information. Thieves love storage units because they are usually easy to break into and have confidential information stored in them.

43. Store all personal information in a secure location in your home, especially if you have roommates.

44. Any company that handles personal information should train all employees, from top to bottom, on responsible information-handling practices.

This information was adapted from http://www.privacyrights.org

CHAPTER 15

SUMMARY – PUTTING IT ALL TOGETHER

To summarize this guide, you have learned some of the things you need to know about repairing your credit rating after you have filed for bankruptcy relief. As you can see, bankruptcy is not the end of the world, and you can have a satisfying, healthy financial life after bankruptcy. You don't have to feel like your life is over just because you filed a bankruptcy case.

In this guide, you learned about the following subjects:

- ☑ Understanding the bankruptcy process

- ☑ Using your home to obtain the credit you need

- ☑ Using prepaid credit cards to get your credit back on track

☑ Avoiding the common scams and lies that are out there for you

☑ Using your home's equity to put you on the right track

☑ The difference between Chapter 7 and Chapter 13 bankruptcy cases and the pros and cons of filing bankruptcy

☑ The warning signs of identity fraud

☑ Preventing identity fraud

☑ Avoiding the pitfalls of going back into debt

You can use the information you learned in this book to improve your credit score. Even though your bankruptcy filing remains on your credit report for up to 10 years after filing, you can still live your life. The key is to not get into debt over your head again.

Bankruptcy is serious and so are the efforts to get out of bad credit problems. If you follow the instructions in this guide, you will be well on your way to achieving a good credit rating again. While many people need to file for bankruptcy, not everyone knows that they can rebuild their credit afterward. Most people think bankruptcy is a terrible thing that you carry around with you forever. This isn't true. You carry a bankruptcy filing around with you for a few years, but not forever.

Once you have declared bankruptcy, you will find that it will be more difficult to obtain credit for major purchases like houses, cars, and personal loans. It may be difficult, but it is possible. That's the best part. You can rebuild your good credit standing after you have declared bankruptcy.

This has been your comprehensive guide for rebuilding your credit and bouncing back from bankruptcy. You have even learned why filing for bankruptcy relief could be a good thing for you. Although bankruptcy is a last resort for dealing with debt, it doesn't have to be your last stop. You can recover and rebuild with the help of an experienced bankruptcy attorney. I urge you to call my office if you have questions about filing a bankruptcy case to resolve your financial problems.

ABOUT THE AUTHOR

Currently serving as state's attorney for the Mississippi Emergency Management Agency, Randall R. Saxton is the founding attorney of Saxton Law, PLLC, which serves as general counsel for Randall Saxton Real Estate, Inc. and R&S Development, Inc. and practices in the areas of bankruptcy, IRS tax installment agreements, business formation, and estate planning, including wills. Randall also serves as the JAG officer for the Mississippi State Guard, on the Board of Directors of the Madison Chamber of Commerce, and is the author of the fictional thriller, Red Sky Warning. He does volunteer work with the Mission First Legal Aid Clinic, as a Mediator for the Jackson Municipal Court, and as a Community Emergency Response Team member.

Randall is a graduate of Mississippi College, where he majored in History and English, receiving his Bachelor of Science degree in 2006, as well as winning a national championship in powerlifting. He also holds a Master of Social Sciences in Administration of Justice, studying abroad in Montpellier, France, before attending law school at the Mississippi College School of Law, and graduating from there in 2010 as a Doctor of Jurisprudence.

Randall is married to Madeline W. Saxton, Regional Business Development and Marketing Coordinator for Jones Walker, LLP, and is a member of First Baptist Church in Jackson. His family enjoys photography, traveling, and their corgi, Hudson.

FREE BACKGROUND INFORMATION AVAILABLE UPON REQUEST

www.ingramcontent.com/pod-product-compliance
Lightning Source LLC
Chambersburg PA
CBHW060638210326
41520CB00010B/1654